Chasing Rainbows

Nikki Williams

BookLeaf Publishing

Presentation by *BookLeaf Publishing*

Web: www.bookleafpub.com

E-mail: info@bookleafpub.com

ISBN: 978-93-95755-22-1

First edition 2022

For brooklyn xx

Madison and Amelia for being my strength

Olivia for bringing us sunshine

& Jack for being my person.

ACKNOWLEDGEMENT

To Jude for all you are and all you do.

Thankyou for loaning your strength when our faulted ♡ to the universe for gifting me the time to love and hold a angel.

To my sisters in many forms, thank you for showing me love, walking beside me, holding my umbrella and showing me the colours that still exsisted in the world.

PREFACE

This collection of poems came to be as a form of writting therapy as i now travel the road as a bereaved mum.
I had days where i didnt want to get out of bed but i had to, i was still a mum to two amazing beautiful strong but confused children who needed their mum as much i needed to be with them.
I have chosen to share my collection with hope that my words can help another parent on their own bereavement journey ♡ if that is you, kind and gentle thoughts are with you on your journey ♡ from my heart to yours x

Healing

Healing is messy,
Healing is hard,
Healing is scary,
Healing's an art.

Hurting is harder,
It brings so much stress.
Its really messy,
And leaves you depressed.

Healing takes strength,
Healing takes power.
To stay soft and sweet,
Not bitter or sour

Healing means dropping,
All of the crap.
That you carry through life,
Slung over your back.

It's putting it down,
It's walking away.
It's saying I'm done,
With living this way!

My fear should not hold me,

My life to embrace.
To let it control me,
would be such a waste.

SIDS

SIDS is a demon,
It brings hell to earth.
A mysterious death
For a baby you birthed.

There's no rhyme or reason,
There isn't any sign.
With all the years of research
Still No answers they can find.

All I get is four letters
What do they mean?
For I lost my baby,
Somewhere deep in her dream.

She slipped away silently,
So beautiful and still,
SIDS is unexpected.
BUT sadly is real.

Forced with a good-bye
Before you had grown.
I would have stayed awake,
If only I'd known.

No tomorrow for us
There was no guarantee.
Now I mourn my baby
And the person she would be.

BROOKLYN JEAN WILLIAMS
31-12-2020 - 21-04-2021

The Questions

No one could prepare me,
For the questions that still come.
How do I even answer?
I'll forever be your mum.

How many kids do you have?
Is this your only one?
What are their ages?
Are you three and done?

Will you try for number four?
Perhaps a boy maybe?
It always shocks me into place,
How do I mention Number three?

These questions come at random times,
Completely from the blue.
I take a sharp inhale,
Do I dare to mention you?

For it is in a place,
I've forced myself to go,
How much do I tell this person?
Do they really need to know?

Sometimes I just say 3
Because its easier that way
I don't want to break the face
I've put on for that day.

Other times I answer four
Because Brooklyn, she was here
I want to boast like all mums
Because she's very dear.

The questions are not easy,
Sometimes they hurt so bad.
The fact I have to feel this,
Makes me really, really mad...

Unless You've Lost a Baby

I find you by the ocean
As my feet walk through the sand
In every little seashell
I put within my hand
The waves softly sing your name
The sun is shining bright
And in that single second
Things still feel alright.

My thoughts are free and breezy
My heart beats a steady pace
I imagine you an angel
I can see your pretty face.
But then the waves roll on
With a bigger one behind
And my mind begins to race
And my thoughts are not so kind.

What if, but why, but how?
The questions start the same
Round and round they go
In the lonely grieving lane.
Grief is like the ocean
The waves roll on each day
But each one is still different

In the most peculiar way.

Sometimes the waves are huge
Sometimes they swoosh in small
Somedays I can take on the world
And other days I fall.
Some days all I have left
Is the pain within my heart
It reminds me we were bound
And will never truly part.

But each day I must keep going on
For I'm a mum of three
I'll always be your mummy
And you'll always be with me.

Primary Loss vs Secondary Loss

The question I have
Is, which is worse?
Secondary loss
Or the loss that comes first
Primary loss, your world falls apart,
It cuts like a knife and it shatters your heart.

But the secondary loss,
Is far-reaching too.
For it's never-ending,
In all that you do.

It's the empty space,
That can never be filled
It's the hole in the heart,
that can never be healed

It's the hopes and the dreams
The wishes and plans
It's the future that's ripped
Right out of our hands

Who you would be?
What would you be like?

Here with your sisters,
To bicker and fight!

The secondary loss,
Is in all that you do.
But the primary loss
Changes all that you knew.

The Primal Cry

The cry is primal,
From the depth of her soul.
The scream that sounds
When she loses control.

The cry that belongs,
To a mother bereaved,
At the foot of a bed,
For the baby she grieves.

The pain can be heard,
In the noises she makes.
As her world falls apart,
And her heart starts to break.

Ripped open a wound,
That can never be healed
A loss from her arms
That can never be filled.

She sobs for her baby
She sobs for her dreams
The is something so primal
That is there in the screams.

I Am Angry, God

I told God I am angry,
That he broke my heart.
Why take my baby?
We were not meant to part.

I told God I was angry,
As I questioned why?
Does he not love me?
Why did my baby die?

I told God I was angry,
He stole my baby from me.
He said "my child I hold her
If only you could see.
She's my brightest Angel
A gem on my knee.
I will hold her safe
Until you visit me"

I told God I was angry,
I yelled with all my might
I broke, I bent, I felt alone
Until I saw his light

I told God I was angry,

He said "my child, it's alright
I'll find a way to heal you
And be your guiding light"

Trust in the higher power,
Thats all that I can say.
He gives you what you can handle,
And will help you find a way.

He loves me and my baby
This I know for sure
He's waiting for me in heaven,
And she'll greet me at the door.

We will be together,
When my days are done.
She'll forever be my baby,
And I'll always be her mum.

The Day I Became a Grieving Mother

The day my baby died,
A piece of me died too.
I became a different person
Something strange and new.

I'm not the woman I once was,
And will never be the same
The only thing that hasn't changed
Is the spelling of my name.

Every day I'm wishing
That I could turn back time
To wake up from this nightmare
Where you are no longer mine.

My heart is now so heavy
The pain is just too raw
I cry much more often
Than I ever did before.

A mother gives herself away
And loves you like no other,
On the day my child died.
I became a grieving mother.

One in Four

Miscarriage, stillbirth and infant loss
Not all pregnancies go to plan,
Having a baby isn't easy
Some need a helping hand.

But when you're 1 in 4
It's hard to stand the pain,
Once you've lost a baby
You will never be the same.

The world's a little colder,
From the place where you once stood.
What a heartbreaking journey
Is this road to motherhood.

But for some reason, it's still taboo
This happens every day!
We see the courage it takes to try again
Knowing it may end this way

You're braver than a warrior,
You're fiercer than a bear
All you really focus on
Is having a baby there

For you so want to be a mum
And hold your baby close
You focus all your energy
On the thing that you want most

But it may never happen
And then you have to find a way
To get up out of bed
And face the world each day

The anger that you feel,
When you see a pregnant mum.
When something that seems so simple,
Is unachievable for some.

So Mumma I see your journey
I feel the pain within your heart
Join the groups no one wants to join
And they'll be there from the start

We are all bereaved mothers
We can help to share your pain.
Love & inspiration from others
Is what you have to gain.

For we've created a choir of angels
Unintentional as that may be
They're singing loud and flying free
In perfect harmony

For Madison My Pretty Girl

When I tell you you're pretty,
What I mean to say.
Is you're pretty amazing,
In every single way.
You are pretty special,
You are one of a kind
You are pretty unique
And you're pretty devine.
You're pretty smart
And you're pretty funny
You're pretty wild,
I'm glad that I'm your mummy.
Your mind is pretty awesome,
How you figure out some stuff
Life can be hard
but you're built pretty tough.
I don't think much will stop you
You're steadfast in what you do.
You're pretty sassy
You're pretty stubborn to boot
And sometimes I mean pretty
Cos you're pretty darn cute
♡♡♡♡♡♡♡♡♡♡♡♡♡♡♡

What I Sent to Heaven

I sent a message to heaven,
I hope it got to you alright.
It was all my love and a hug,
So you know you're on my mind.

I sent a wish to heaven,
It was all my hopes and dreams.
That you are loved & cared for,
And paradise is all it seems.

I sang a song to heaven,
Can you hear my melody?
The songs within my heart,
That have bonded you to me

I whispered up to heaven,
My girl, I miss you so
I'll never really understand,
Why God needed you to go.

I waved up to heaven,
Can you see me from the clouds?
I told you that I love you,
I yelled it really loud.

I sent a prayer to heaven
To remind God how precious you are,
And to give me strength on my journey,
Of loving you from afar. ♡♡♡

Earth Side Daughters

For my two girls, I must do it.
For my girls, I stay strong.
Even when everything,
Still feels so wrong.

I must harvest my pain
I must keep pushing on,
For I am the place,
Where you truly belong.

You give me strength,
You help make it right,
And crawl into my bed for a snuggle at night,
Your look for me,
When you're tired and sad
You look for me,
when life makes you mad.

When you want to be silly,
You come and find me,
Your silly place is where
I want to be.
Your mind is amazing
You blow me away,
With your games and your thoughts,

That you have every day.
You are funny and cheeky,
Two sweet little ones
Life with you is a wonder
And you make it so fun.

I'm your biggest fan,
I'll always cheer you on,
Whether you get it right
or when you get it wrong
I will love and support you,
This I promise to you
I will have your back
In whatever you do.

For you are my child
Second to none
And I promise a kiss goodnight
When your day is done
And in the morning
We have cuddles and kisses galore
For you are my babies
The ones I adore ♡

Vilomah

People always ask
Are you doing ok?
My usual answer is sure
But what I mean to say
Is, this is such a challenge
To navigate this road
And the grief that I carry
Is such a heavy load

I want to speak her name
To hear it said out loud,
I want to boast like all mums
Cos I was really proud
Now it seems so empty
There's a hole inside my heart
How do you begin to heal?
Where do you even start?

There is no word for where I am
In death, there are a few.
A husbandless wife is a widow,
And a husband a widower too.
A parentless child is an orphan,
But where does that leave me?
Vilomah?? For it is un-natural

And not how that it should be.
Now I've lost a child
I'm a completely different me,
Who will become this person?
I have to wait and see!
But meantime I will strive
To be the best human I can be.

Conversation with the Bereaved

I lost a baby
I hear myself say
The person I'm telling
just turns away
I don't know why I said
Not to make them feel bad

But I need them to know
My heart's really sad.
I've lost something so precious and so very dear
I need them to know my baby was here.
She was so wanted
And she was so loved
But now she has gone from my world,
She's in heaven above.

I don't know how to live
Without my baby with me
At times it's so dark
It's impossible to see
How do I live
When I lost part of me?

In me she grew

My body her home
Now this world
Is empty and alone

3 living children
For me to adore
But my heart is still shattered
All over the floor.
It burst into pieces
It ripped at the seams
Nothing is as important
As it once seemed to have been

It all seems too trivial
Wrapped up in guff
Surviving each day
Is really quiet tough

I play the part
I laugh and I smile,
But my heart it is broken
And it will be for a while

It's not something I can turn off
My head filled with fear
It takes time they said
We're in our first year
It's almost a year since my baby was here.

A year of firsts
Filled with pain that's still raw
How do I go back
To who I was before?

Before all the trauma
Before all the pain
I know that my world
Will never be the same
I have to find a space
Where grief can exist
While taking in life
And enjoying the bits
But that is a place
Which feels hard to find
In my year of firsts
Where my thoughts are unkind

Take it minute by minute
Do the best I can do.
Whilst remembering my love
And honouring you.

Dreaming

In my dreams,
you visit me
I see your face,
As clear as can be.
Your beautiful smile
And your head full of hair
In your eyes
I could just sit and stare
I scoop you up
I cuddle and kiss
I feel a moment of pure bliss
This is pure love
And there's nothing to say
My only wish
Is to stay this way.
But alas I must awake
To the crushing reality
That is my fate
That up in heaven
You must wait.

Until that day,
When I come to find you.
When I've finished this journey
And paid all my dues

Your face will be the first I find
And we wait together
For those behind
We'll All be together again one day
You see Heaven is not too far away
Till then
I will wait for you
In my sleep
My heart wide open
For you to seek.
You're dancing with me
In my dreams
I love you forever
My Brooklyn Jean

You should be here

You should be here
This wasn't the plan
You should be here
Holding my hand
I miss you so much
The pain runs so deep
When I think what I've lost
I sit and I weep
You should be here
It can't be undone
You should be here
You are second to none
Robbed of the life
We all could have had
My mind's going crazy
My heart's really sad

Disassociation

When you don't know where you're going,
And you don't know where you've been,
Sometimes with disassociation,
It feels like living in a dream.

The pain is sometimes numbing
Sometimes I don't feel a thing
other times my heart aches
With the pain only grief can bring.

It's totally consuming
It's easier to just switch off
It's so much easier to disassociate
Than it is coping with the loss

So if I seem forgetful,
Please remember to be kind,
It is never my intention.
a lot plays on my mind.

If I seem unfriendly,
Please know that that's not me.
Sit with me a while,
My kindness you will see.

If I don't reply,
To the text that you have sent,
Please know
I'm not avoiding you,
But my energy's been spent.

Thanks to those who listen,
To the ones that lend an ear.
Thanks for sitting in my grief,
It's nice to have you here.

Mother's day

Mothers day feels different
Its bittersweet for me
Im a mum of four
But only have three of them with me.
I want to celebrate my children
And im proud to be their mum
But my heart will forever break
For im missing a little one.
So if you wish me happy mothers day
Please remember to be kind
Please mention my baby
We both know shes on my mind ♡

Oh, Heart!

He's off to work
He pays the bills
Her days at home
8 hours to fill
But she's up at night
This is the deal?

Turning up, getting down
Petty words, resentments found
No more sleeping in
Once spent together
No days off
When she's under the weather

Not a drop, to blow off steam
Her social life
Lives in her dreams
Shopping trips
A task to do
Someone always needing you
Lunches to make
They need breakfast too
Wishing there were two of you.

Pass the baton

I'm lucky for an hour
Right, it's your turn
I'm off to the shower.

But at the end of the day
It's me and you
I guess what I'm saying
Is, I"m missing just us two

I remember it well
That adolescent love of ours
Carefree and easy
Chilling for hours.

I wouldn't change it
Life's better with them
But I guess
I just miss you
and I miss where we've been

Today

Today my heart is heavy
Today I hold back tears
Today I relive losing you
And I'm filled with so much fear.

Today I miss you dearly
Today I'm wanting you
How I long to celebrate you
As most mums get to do.

Today my soul is tired
From keeping me afloat
Today I wish I could speak to you in person
But instead to you,
Another letter wrote.

Today was a little harder
Today hurts a little more
I get to hug my little 3
But I'm wishing it were 4.

Today is filled with love
Today I hold no space for tears
Today I find a space for you
To honour you my dear

Today I miss you, baby
And every day its always there
Today I feel you darling
And all the love that we got to share

I'm thinking of every day I had
To hold you in my arms
Today I feel your presence near
Today I'll find a gentle calm.

My Shadows

I saw a mum,
With tired eyes.
With 3 little kids,
She had in sight.

She was trying to keep them,
There by her side.
One racing ahead,
One lagging behind,
Another worn in a carrier sort,
While she balanced the bags,
Of things she had bought.

"You've got your hand full"
I say with a smile
"With three little ones
Your day must seem wild"

She says
"I'm glad for my shadows,
It means I have sun,
I'm grateful to have,
these 3 little ones.
They keep my days full,
Of love and of laughter.

My 3 little shadows,
For me to look after,
You see I've known joy,
But I've also known sadness
Sometimes I get overwhelmed,
In all of the madness,
But at the end of the day,
I'm grateful they're mine
And I wouldn't give up,
This moment in time."

www.ingramcontent.com/pod-product-compliance
Lightning Source LLC
Chambersburg PA
CBHW051741130826
49812CB00033B/960
9789395755221